Balloons are floating in the sky,
Pretty colors, passing by.
Big balloons in sunny weather,
How many are there altogether?

Find the groups, and then you'll see.
The answer comes so easily.

Here are some riddles to make adding fun,
And quicker than counting things one by one.
Find a group, or find a pair,
Then add the groups that you see there.

Sunflowers grow up very tall.
How many sunflowers are there in all?
As they reach out to the sun,
There's no need to count each one.

Find the groups, and then you'll see.
The answer comes so easily.

Math Riddles

by Susan Ring

STECK-VAUGHN
Harcourt Supplemental Publishers

www.steck-vaughn.com

There are **three** groups of **two** sunflowers.
You can count the sunflowers by **twos.**

$$2 + 2 + 2 = 6$$

Or you can multiply.

$$3 \times 2 = 6$$

There are six sunflowers in all.

There are **three** groups of **three** balloons.
You can count the balloons by **threes.**

$$3 + 3 + 3 = 9$$

Or you can multiply.

$$3 \times 3 = 9$$

There are nine balloons in all.

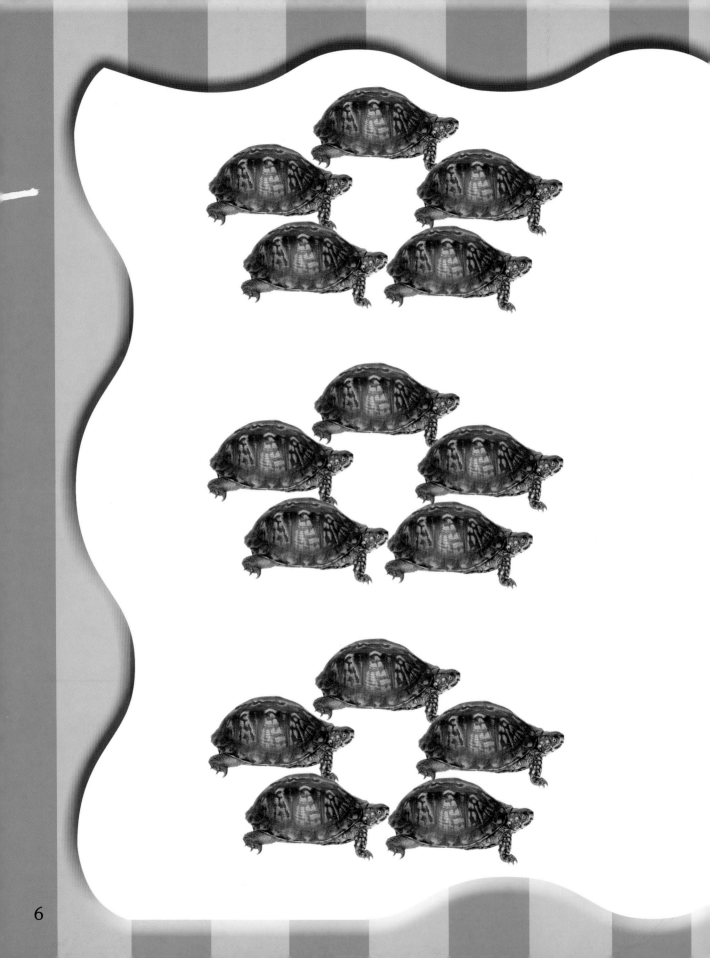

Turtles come to say hello.
How many are there? Do you know?
Instead of counting every one,
Find the groups. That makes it fun!

Find the groups, and then you'll see.
The answer comes so easily.

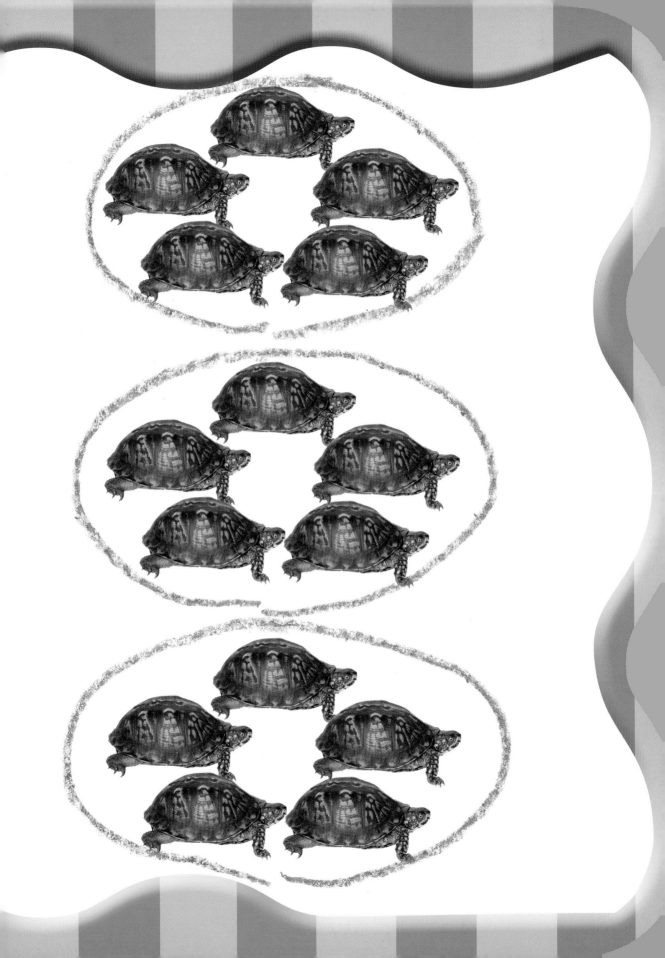

There are **three** groups of **five** turtles.
You can count the turtles by **fives.**

$$5 + 5 + 5 = 15$$

Or you can multiply.

$$3 \times 5 = 15$$

There are fifteen turtles in all.

Flying moths, with their spots,
Can you count all of the dots?
To make it easy, here's a clue,
These dots come in groups of two.

Find the groups, and then you'll see.
The answer comes so easily.

There are four moths.
Each moth has two spots.
There are **four** groups of **two** dots.
You can count the dots by **twos.**

$$2 + 2 + 2 + 2 = 8$$

Or you can multiply.

$$4 \times 2 = 8$$

There are eight dots in all.

Cherries are a tasty treat.
How many cherries are there to eat?
You can count them one by one,
But which way is a lot more fun?

Find the groups, and then you'll see.
The answer comes so easily.

There are **five** groups of **three** cherries.
You can count the cherries by **threes.**

$$3+3+3+3+3=15$$

Or you can multiply.

$$5 \times 3 = 15$$

There are fifteen cherries in all.

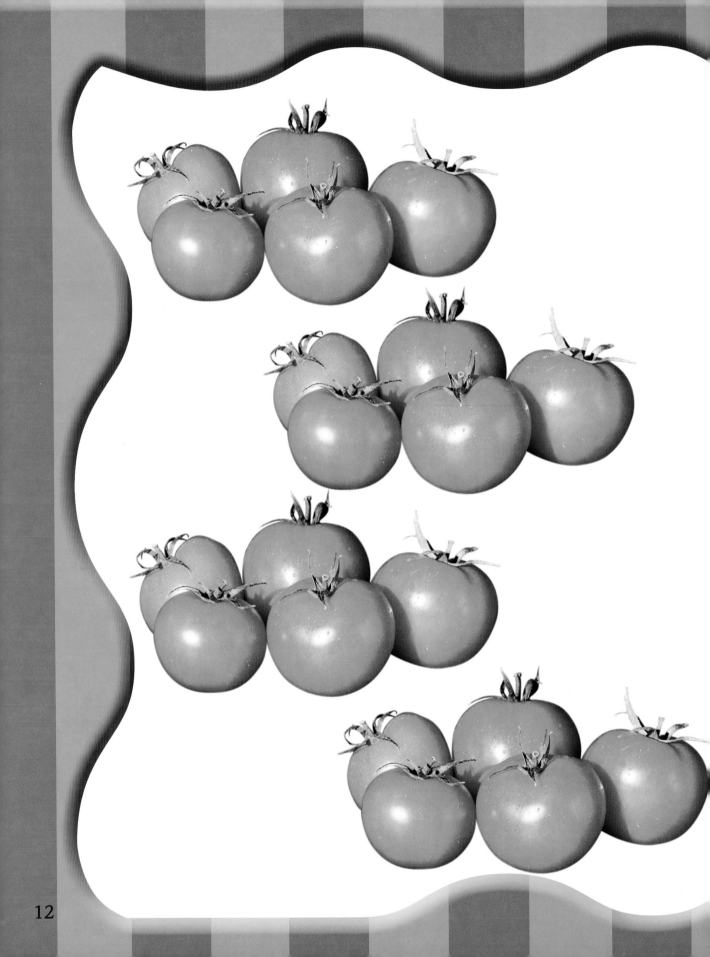

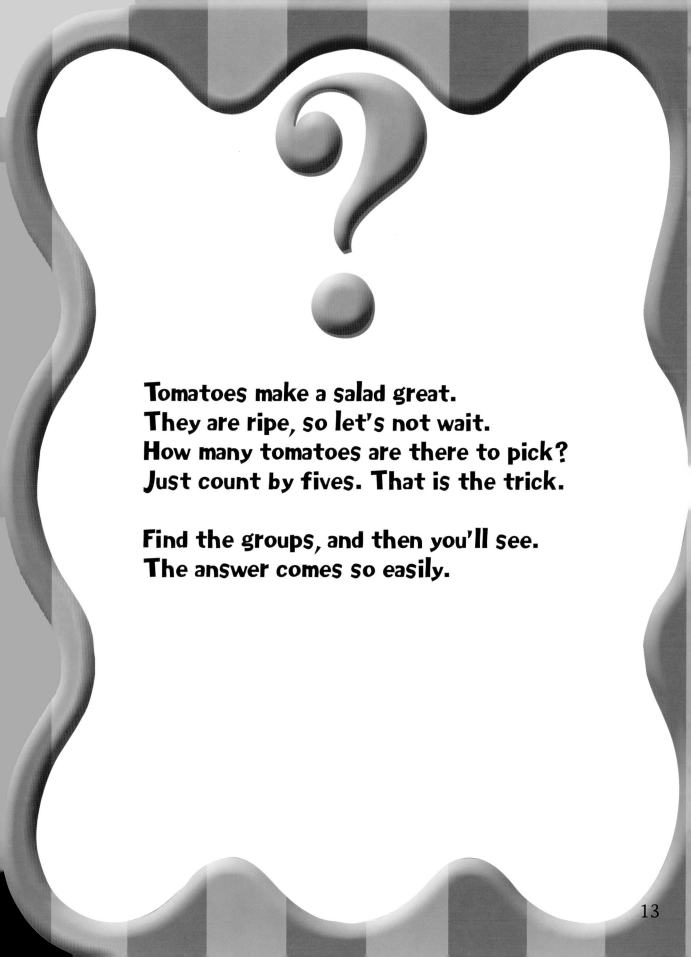

Tomatoes make a salad great.
They are ripe, so let's not wait.
How many tomatoes are there to pick?
Just count by fives. That is the trick.

Find the groups, and then you'll see.
The answer comes so easily.

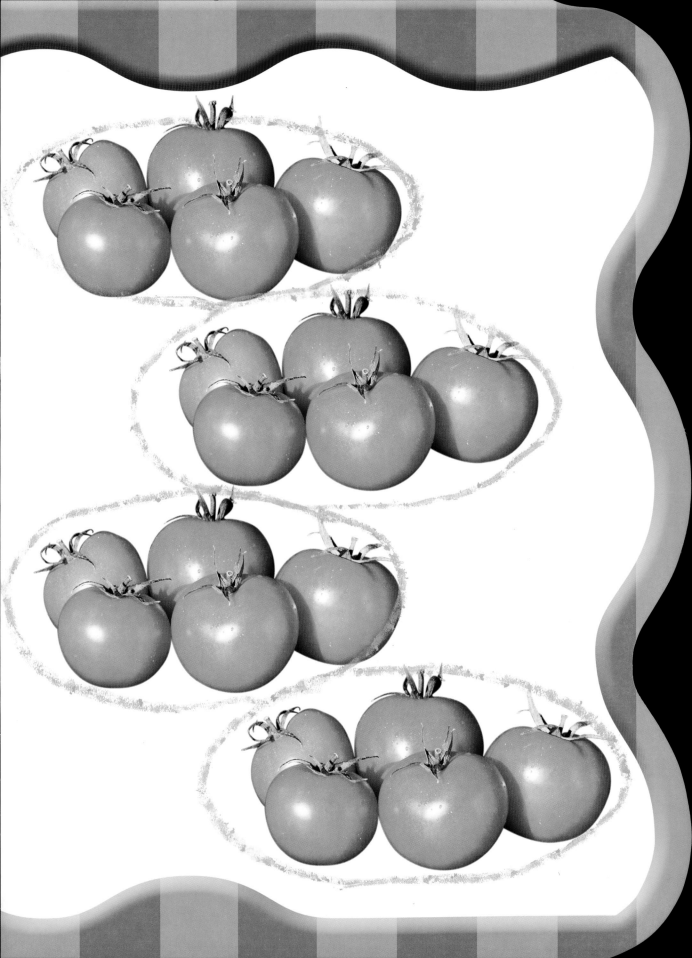

There are **four** groups of **five** tomatoes.
You can count the tomatoes by **fives.**

$$5 + 5 + 5 + 5 = 20$$

Or you can multiply.

$$4 \times 5 = 20$$

There are twenty tomatoes in all.

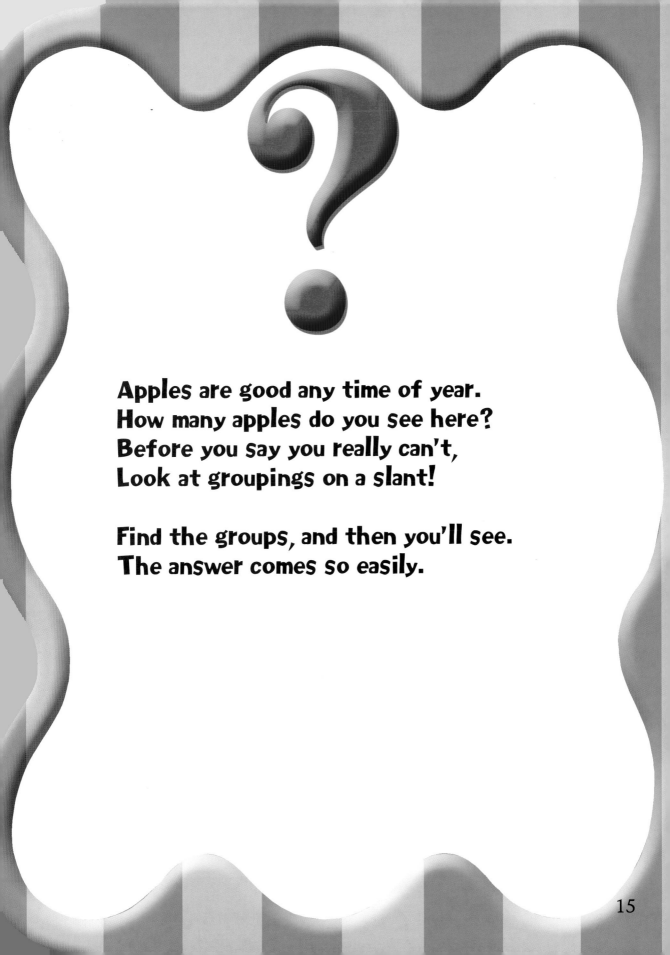

Apples are good any time of year.
How many apples do you see here?
Before you say you really can't,
Look at groupings on a slant!

Find the groups, and then you'll see.
The answer comes so easily.

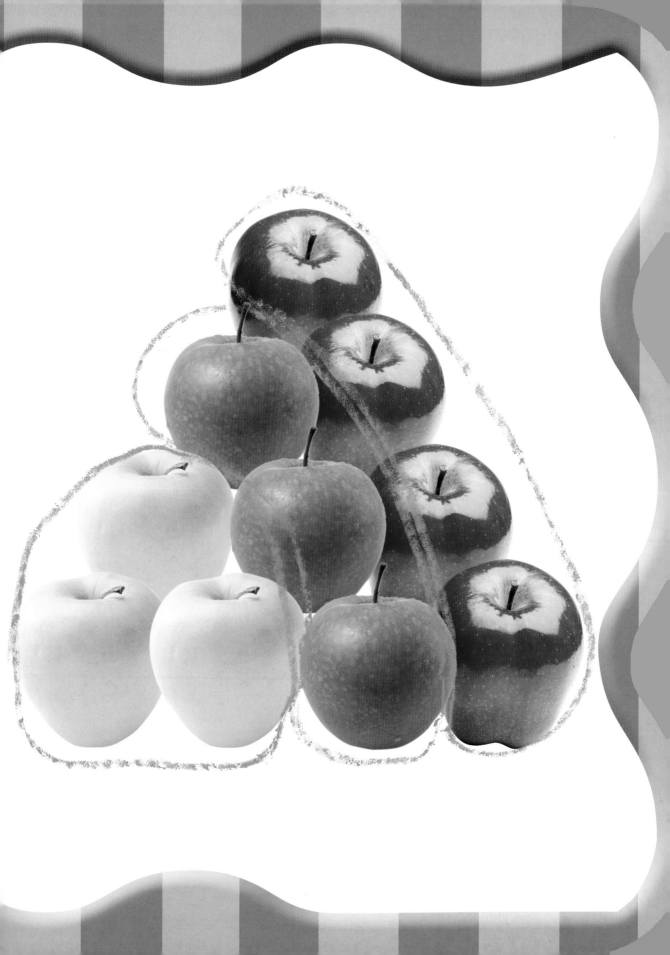

There are two groups of three apples.
Three plus **three** equals **six.**

$$3 + 3 = 6$$

There is one more group of four apples.
Six plus **four** equals **ten.**

$$6 + 4 = 10$$

There are ten apples in all.

Beetles scurry on the ground.
There are beetles all around.
So get your toes out of the way,
As you count the beetles today.

Find the groups, and then you'll see.
The answer comes so easily.

There is one group of two beetles.
There is one group of four beetles.
Two plus **four** equals **six**.

$$2 + 4 = 6$$

There is one more group of three beetles.
Six plus **three** equals **nine**.

$$6 + 3 = 9$$

There are nine beetles in all.

Here is a large group of fish.
You can count them, if you wish.
But to count them really fast,
Use addition—it's a blast!

Find the groups, and then you'll see.
The answer comes so easily.

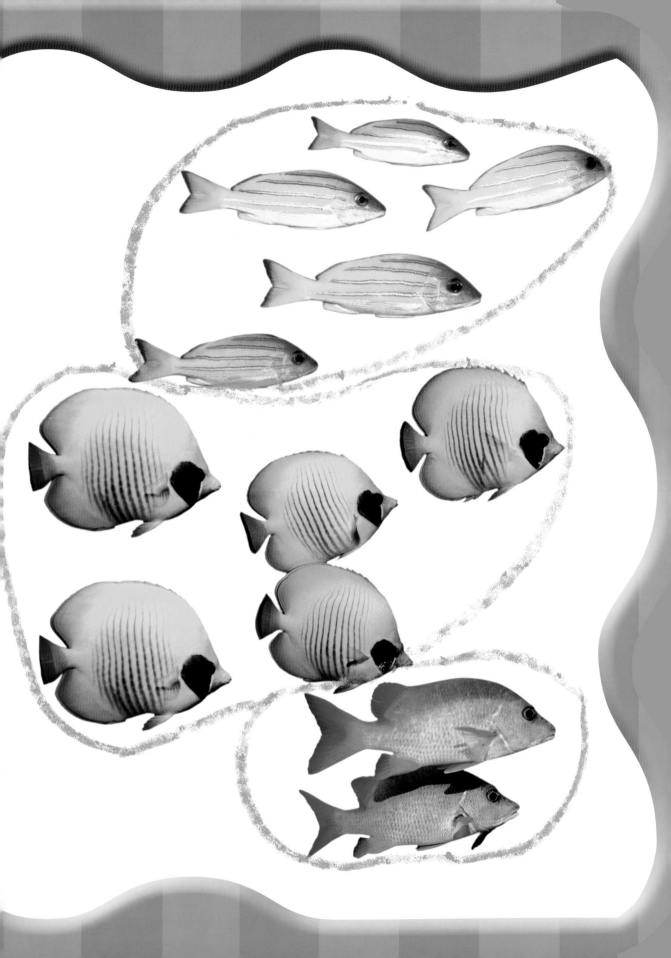

There are two groups of five fish.
Five plus **five** equals **ten.**

$$5 + 5 = 10$$

There is one more group of two fish.
Ten plus **two** equals **twelve.**

$$10 + 2 = 12$$

There are twelve fish in all.

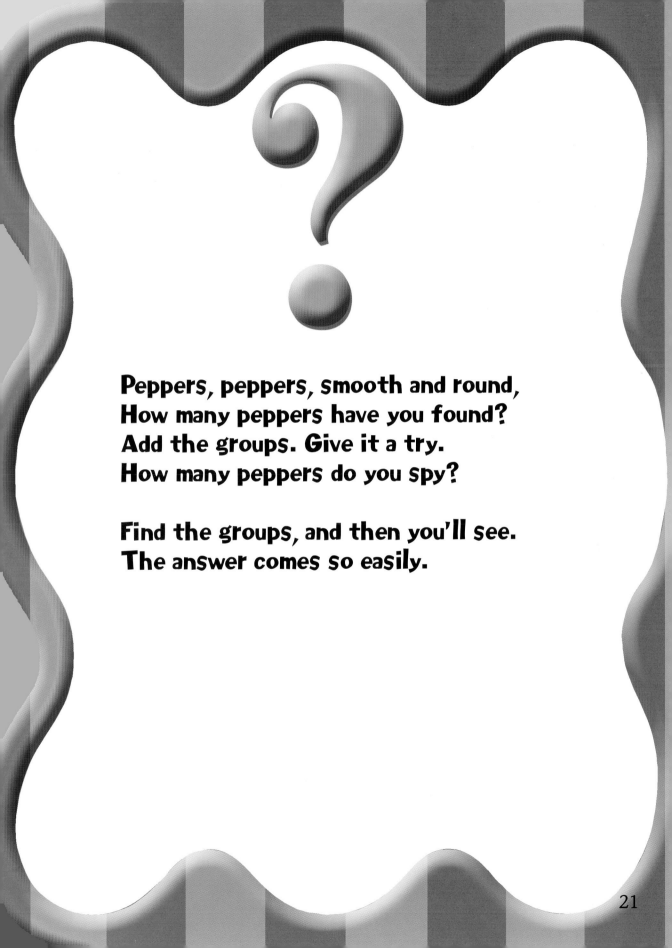

Peppers, peppers, smooth and round,
How many peppers have you found?
Add the groups. Give it a try.
How many peppers do you spy?

Find the groups, and then you'll see.
The answer comes so easily.

There is one group of three green peppers.
There is one group of four yellow peppers.
Three plus **four** equals **seven.**

$$3 + 4 = 7$$

There is one more group of six red peppers.
Seven plus **six** equals **thirteen.**

$$7 + 6 = 13$$

There are thirteen peppers in all.

Butterflies float in the sky.
In groups of color, they flutter by.
How many butterflies can be seen,
If first you add the blue and green?

Find the groups, and then you'll see.
The answer comes so easily.

There is one group of six green butterflies.
There is one group of five blue butterflies.
Six plus five equals eleven.

$$6 + 5 = 11$$

There is one more group of four yellow butterflies.
Eleven plus four equals fifteen.

$$11 + 4 = 15$$

There are fifteen butterflies in all.

How many shells are on the beach?
Can you tell without counting each?
Find the groups, and then you'll see.
The answer comes so easily.

24